The Ancient
CHINESE

Revised and Updated

JANE SHUTER

Heinemann Library
Chicago, Illinois

© 1998, 2007 Heinemann Library
a division of Reed Elsevier Inc.
Chicago, Illinois

Customer Service 888-454-2279
Visit our website at www.heinemannraintree.com

Designed by Richard Parker and Q2A Solutions
Printed in China by WKT Company Ltd

11 10 09 08 07
10 9 8 7 6 5 4 3 2 1

New edition ISBNs:
1-403-48809-6 (hardback)
1-403-48816-9 (paperback)

13 digit ISBNs:
978-1-403-48809-1 (hardback)
978-1-403-48816-9 (paperback)

The Library of Congress has cataloged the first edition as follows:
Shuter, Jane.
    The ancient Chinese / Jane Shuter.
    p.   cm. — (History opens windows)
    Includes bibliographical references and index.
    Summary: An introduction to the various elements of ancient Chinese civilization, including
    great thinkers, family life, inventions, and the government.
    ISBN 1-57572-593-2 (lib. bdg.)   ISBN 1-57572-594-0 (pbk.)
    1. China—Civilization—Juvenile literature.
    2. China—History—Juvenile literature.
     [1. China—Civilization.]   I Title. II. Series.
    DS721 .S488   1998
    951—dc21
                                    97-35801
                                       CIP
                                       AC

Acknowledgments
The author and publishers are grateful to the following for permission to reproduce copyright
photographs:Ancient Art & Architecture Collection Ltd., p. **7**, **12**, **27**; Bibliotheque Nationale,
Paris, p. **8**; British Museum, p. **10**, **13**, **14**, **16**, **17**, **20**, **28**; Smithsonian, Freer Art Gallery,
Washington DC, p. **18**, **26**; The Museum of Fine Arts, Boston, p. **21**; WM Rockhill Nelson Gall, p.
22; National Palace Museum, Taiwan, p. **24**.

Cover photograph reproduced with permission of AKG-Images / Laurent Lecat.

Contents

Some words are shown in bold, **like this**.
You can find out what they mean by looking in the glossary.

Introduction

This map shows Ancient China at its biggest under the Han dynasty in about 100 BC.

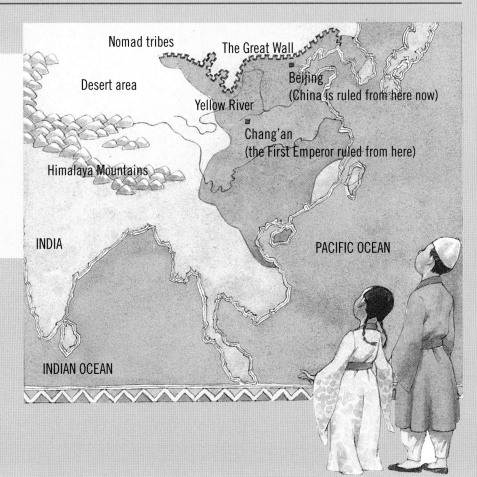

Nomad tribes

The Great Wall

Beijing
(China is ruled from here now)

Desert area

Yellow River

Chang'an
(the First Emperor ruled from here)

Himalaya Mountains

INDIA

PACIFIC OCEAN

INDIAN OCEAN

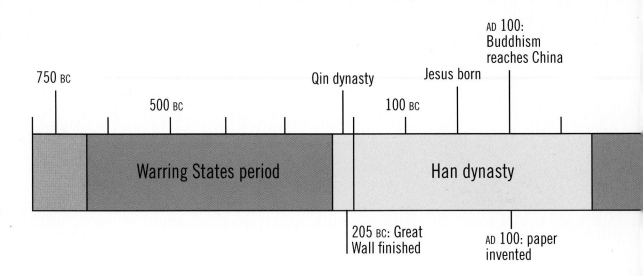

AD 100: Buddhism reaches China

750 BC

Qin dynasty

Jesus born

500 BC

100 BC

Warring States period

Han dynasty

205 BC: Great Wall finished

AD 100: paper invented

4

People first lived in China about 500,000 years ago. They hunted and then farmed along the Huang He (pronounced "hwong hee"), also called the Yellow River. Historians divide ancient Chinese history into dynasties, which are blocks of time when China was ruled by different families. Each dynasty is named after the ruling family.

The first two Chinese dynasties, the Shang and the Zhou (pronounced "Jo"), ruled from 1700 BC to 770 BC. But the Zhou dynasty lost control. Families that ruled different parts of China fought for power. This period, called the Warring States, lasted 600 years. Finally, the Qin (pronounced "chin") dynasty won. From then on, China was ruled by one Chinese dynasty after another until the Mongols invaded in 1279.

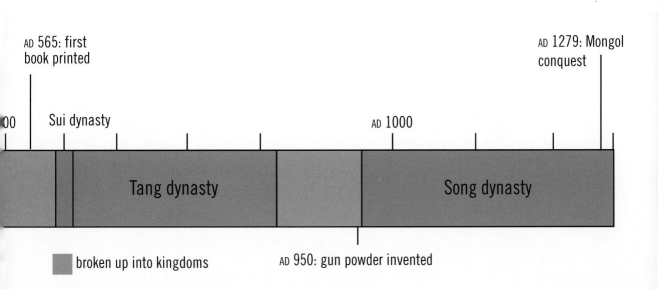

AD 565: first book printed

AD 1279: Mongol conquest

00 Sui dynasty

AD 1000

Tang dynasty

Song dynasty

broken up into kingdoms

AD 950: gun powder invented

The First Emperor

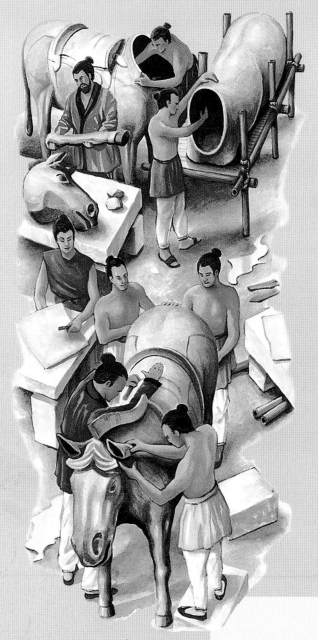

Shi Huangdi (pronounced "She hwong dee"), leader of the Qin, renamed himself "the First **Emperor**" because he wanted his dynasty to make a new start after the Warring States period. His **empire** was bigger than any earlier empire. He was the first ruler to try to make China one country.

Earlier rulers had let different parts of their empire live differently. The First Emperor did not. He made people use the same writing, the same coins, and the same weights and measures in the markets. He even made them make carts the same size to fit the new roads that were being built all over the empire.

The First Emperor wanted a great burial. For years before his death, workers made a huge terra-cotta (pottery) army to guard his tomb. Here they are making horses.

Here are a few of the 7,000 terra-cotta warriors who guarded the First Emperor's tomb. They were made with great care. No two of them are exactly the same.

How China Was Ruled

This painting shows the First Emperor reading the names of the men who have passed the test to become a government official.

The First **Emperor** wanted to control the **empire**. So he set up a system of officials to run the country. There were officials to run the army and also officials to organize common citizens. These officials collected **taxes**, checked markets, and punished criminals. This system was used for many years. Only men could become officials. They had to pass a set of tests that were held every three years. For each person who passed, about 3,000 failed.

In ancient China, the emperor was the most important person. He owned all the land. Everyone had to obey him. After him came the **nobles**. These were rich and important Chinese families. Next were scholars, who studied and wrote books—education and knowledge were very important to the ancient Chinese. Next came the farmers who kept everyone fed. The least important people were shopkeepers, **craftworkers**, and then **merchants**.

Only an emperor's family, nobles, and important officials could talk directly to him.

Religion

Ancient Chinese religion had many different parts. Sometimes it is hard to separate them from each other. One of the most important parts for many common people involved the spirits and demons that affected everyday life.

There were spirits of nature and of different parts of life, such as wealth, health, children, and happiness. All these spirits had to be kept happy.

The Guardian King of the North controlled the north point of the compass. He was just one of the many spirits and demons that could change everyday life.

The ancient Chinese also worshiped the spirits of their parents, grandparents, great-grandparents, and other **ancestors**. On special days in spring and fall, everyone spent time at **temples** or family shrines to worship their ancestors.

From the first century AD, the emperors were interested in Buddhism. They heard about it by trading with India, where Buddhism began. Buddhists believed in **meditation** and **reincarnation**.

People worshiped at this huge statue of Buddha, carved into a mountain.

Great Thinkers

Confucius taught in about 500 BC. One of his most important ideas was that a person should obey and respect people who are older and more important. The First **Emperor** burned Confucius' writings because he wanted to make a new start. Years later, followers of Confucius spread his teachings. Confucius' ideas became popular once again.

Lao Tzu (Lao rhymes with "cow," and Tzu is pronounced "Sue") lived at about the same time as Confucius. He told people to **meditate** on the "Tao," or "Way." He said all living things should work together in harmony.

Confucius said every group of people, from families to countries, had to follow this rule: "Obey more important people and take care of less important people."

Lao Tzu's ideas about the Way, or Tao, later became a religion called Taoism.

Country Life

Most common Chinese people lived and worked in the countryside. They grew different crops. In the north they grew grain, such as wheat and **millet**. In the south where it was wetter, farmers grew rice. Most people grew vegetables and kept chickens and pigs. Oxen and buffalo pulled their plows and carts.

In spring, the **emperor** was the first to plow a field. This showed that farming was very important. But even though farmers were important to the **empire**, they were usually the poorest people in it.

Rice must be underwater for part of its growing time, so rice fields need to be near rivers. Here farmers move water from the river to the paddy field with a bamboo scoop.

A Guarded Village from the Time of the First Emperor

The lord's cart is pulled by horses. Common villagers might share one or two buffaloes or oxen to pull their carts and plows.

Common people live in these one-roomed thatched houses.

The well is where all the water comes from, including drinking water for humans and animals.

The lord of the land all around the village has a house in this village.

Town Life

The size and design of cities showed how powerful an **emperor** was. New emperors often had a capital city built to rule from. These cities were carefully planned, with the emperor's palace and the government offices at the end farthest from the poor parts of the city.

Other cities and towns were carefully planned, too. Many had big market places and special streets set aside for different businesses. Smaller towns grew bit by bit. They had many wood houses on narrow, twisting streets. These houses could catch fire and burn down very easily.

Farmers brought their extra crops to market to sell. They shared an ox cart, like the one in this model, to carry the crops.

A Busy Town Market

This man has just sold his sheep.

This man is telling stories.

Traders have set up stalls on the bridge.

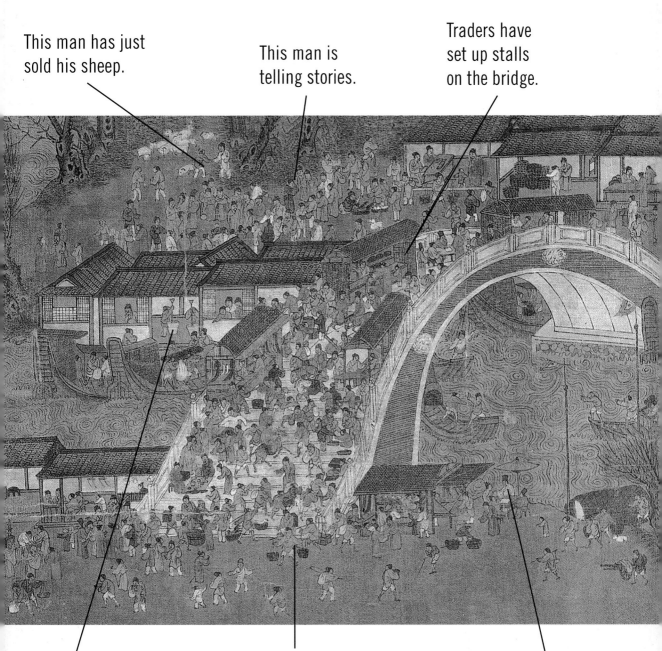

People are dyeing silk in this workshop.

Villagers without carts carry baskets on bamboo poles over their shoulders.

This scholar makes his living writing letters for people.

Family Life

Women in rich families had no work to do, but did not often go out. So they had to entertain each other with games, singing, and talking.

The ancient Chinese had very clear ideas about how a family should live. The father was the head of the family. Everyone had to obey him, even his grown-up children. Confucius taught that people should be more respected as they grew older. So the oldest members of the family were well cared for.

Men worked and did business outside the home. Most women ran the home and looked after the children. Women who were very poor worked in the fields or as servants in wealthier homes.

18

The House of a Wealthy Chinese Family

Even wealthy people had very little furniture. The furniture, rugs, and wall hangings they did have were made from expensive woods and fabrics.

The house has a strong wood frame, plastered walls, and a tile roof. Poor people often lived in a one-room house with a straw roof.

The overhanging roof keeps the house cool in the heat and lets water run off when it rains.

Children

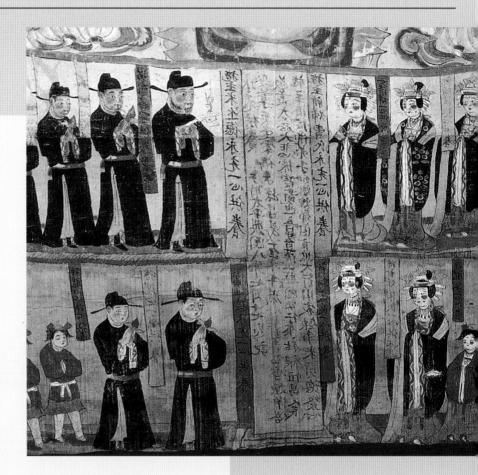

This painting shows a man, his wife, and children, and grandchildren. The writing in the middle is a prayer that says: "There will be many more children and grandchildren, through many generations."

Children were a great blessing, especially boys. People thought that a large family was a good thing. Children were brought up to obey adults.

Boys usually followed their fathers' trades. Wealthy families educated their sons so they could become government officials. Sometimes a wealthy family paid for an intelligent poor boy to be educated to become an official.

Girls were expected to marry, run a home, and have children. Girls from **noble** families might be chosen as one of the **emperor's** many wives. They were well looked after for their entire lives. But they had even less freedom than most Chinese women. They spent almost all their time inside the many palaces that belonged to the emperor.

The girls in this picture are being shown how to make silk. The Chinese were the first to make silk. **Merchants** who sold it all over the world made a lot of money.

Clothes

Wealthy Chinese people wore robes wrapped around and tied at the waist. There were several layers of these robes. The outside layer was always the most beautiful. In summer, the layers were thin. In winter, padding was added between several layers of cloth. Poor people wore trousers and shorter jackets that were practical to work in.

You can see the layers of robes on this statue of a Buddhist priest.

Wealthy people wore long robes made from expensive silk fabrics that were beautifully decorated. There were rules about what colors people could wear. There were special colors for the **emperor**. Poor people wore flat shoes or went barefoot. Wealthy women had their feet bound. Their feet were wrapped tightly in cloth from birth. This broke the bones and made the feet like tiny stumps. Many people thought this looked beautiful.

The emperor and his **nobles** wear richly decorated silk robes. The robes are too long to run or work in. This shows that whoever wears these robes does not work.

The scholar and his wife wear less expensive clothes. But their robes are long, and his shoes have curled toes. They are hard to work or run in.

The farmer's family wear clothes made from inexpensive fabric. These clothes are comfortable to work in.

Food

These people are eating in a garden. There are many bowls with different foods in them. They will eat with the chopsticks next to their plates.

The food that Chinese people ate depended on how wealthy they were.

Poor people did not eat meat every day. They ate chickens that no longer laid eggs. They also hunted and ate wild animals.

Wealthy people ate many kinds of meat, such as pork, chicken, lamb, and goose. On special occasions, they served more unusual things, such as snakes, dogs, snails, and small birds.

Everyone ate vegetables, fruit, and bread. In the south, they ate rice. In the north, people ate a cereal called **millet**. They drank Chinese tea or rice wine. People ate with their fingers or with chopsticks.

A Food Stall in a Small Town

Many people in towns and villages set up food stalls in the street. In some towns, whole streets were lined with different food stalls.

This stall owner has brought a pot of hot food to sell. Other stall owners are cooking over a fire.

This man has bought a large meal and is taking it home on a tray.

This man has bought just a bowl of rice and is eating it while sitting on a mat provided by the stall owner.

Inventions

It was important to be able to raise water, especially in the south where the rice fields needed flooding at times.

The Chinese invented and discovered many things. Many of their inventions were very useful, such as wheelbarrows and writing paper. They also figured out how to move water for farming and how to predict earthquakes. Other inventions include things that made them stronger in war, such as gunpowder and steel for sharper swords.

The Chinese also studied the stars and planets. They invented ways of keeping time. Chinese medicine, especially **acupuncture**, is used by more and more people all over the world today instead of modern medicine.

Some Chinese inventions still in use include: paper, gunpowder, toilet paper, fireworks, umbrellas, kites, wheelbarrows, **abacuses**, canals, and magnetic compasses.

This is a seismographic machine to measure how strong an earthquake is. It was invented by Chang Heng in AD 132. When there was an earthquake, balls fell from the dragons' mouths (at the top) into the toads' mouths (at the bottom).

The Great Wall

The Great Wall was built in the time of the First **Emperor**. It stretched along the northern edge of the Chinese **Empire**. It connected walls built in different places by different dynasties during the Warring States period. The Great Wall was built to keep the Chinese in and the **nomad** tribes that raided from the north out.

The Great Wall was mostly built by the army. But poor farmers and criminals were also forced to work on it. It was not easy to build. So many people died building it that it was called "the longest graveyard in the world."

A pottery model of a watchtower. Watchtowers were built all along the Great Wall.

The Great Wall of China

The parts of the Great Wall that are left stretch for more than 2,100 miles (3,400 kilometers). Historians think it was even longer when it was first built.

Soldiers guard the wall as it is built. They stop enemies from stealing or breaking down the wall. They also stop workers from running away!

Elephants were brought in to help with moving the heaviest loads. But most of the moving is done by humans.

The Mongol Invasion

By AD 1279, the **nomads** in the north, the Mongols, had built themselves into a powerful fighting force. They were building an **empire** of their own. They moved south into China and west into Europe, taking more land than any army before or since. As they took over new lands, they settled and took on the local way of life. Ancient China had come to an end after more than 2,000 years. The Mongol dynasties were just beginning.

Mongol soldiers attack a walled city. They have ladders and a tower to reach the top of the walls.

Glossary

abacus device that uses beads to help add, subtract, multiply, and divide

acupuncture medical treatment in which needles are put into the body at certain points to cure illnesses

ancestors parents, grandparents, great-grandparents, and so on

craftworkers people who make things for a living

emperor ruler who has total power, like a king

empire all the lands controlled by one country

meditation to think about something in a calm, clear way

merchant person who buys things from one person and sells them to others

millet wheat-like grain, used for making bread and beer

noble important person

nomad person who does not live in one place, but moves around

reincarnation belief that a person's soul may be reborn in another body

tax money people pay to support their government

temple place where people worship their gods

Find Out More

Books to read
Hands on Ancient History: Ancient China, Jameson Anderson
   (Heinemann Library, 2006)
DK Eyewitness Books: Ancient China, Arthur Cotterell (Dorling Kindersley, 2005)

Using the Internet
Explore the Internet to find out more about the ancient Chinese. Use a search engine, such as www.yahooligans.com or www.internet4kids.com and type in a keyword or phrase such as "Great Wall of China" or "Confucius".

Index